Kintsugi Through a Kaleidoscope

Kintsugi Through a Kaleidoscope

Ahmed Ayoub

Ahmed Ayoub

*For the lost and unheard trying to find themselves
and words for their feelings.*

Contents

Contents

II.
Messiness

Contents

III.

Rebuilding

Contents

IV.
Scars of Gold

Contents

Preface

Kintsugi [kin-tsoo-gee]

(noun) the Japanese art of repairing broken pottery by mending the areas of breakage with lacquer dusted or mixed with powdered gold, silver, or platinum.

This book was first a dream born in my senior year of high school, and became a goal after so many years. The very existence of this collection is proof that your desires can somehow, one day, overcome the very themes and emotions contained within these pages. Like the concept of kintsugi, people are just as beautiful because of their struggles and imperfections, rather than in spite of them. This book aims to convey that.

While I write from my own thoughts, experiences, or feelings as an Egyptian Muslim man born in the United States, I hope that through this journey you find something that makes you feel less alone, as the world can be incredibly lonely when you can't find words to match your state of being. May this book of mine encourage you to find, craft, or empower your own voice. Bismillah.

I.

The Fall and Fracture

Stolen Dreams

The bittersweet dream of most children of
the diaspora
is that
we aspire to be painters,
Writers,
Artists,
Actors, and dancers.
But are instead forced into molds of
Our ancestors' pride and strife;

You can be anything you want habibi,
As long as it's a
Lawyer,
Doctor,
Or engineer.

Diamonds may be formed under pressure but our
Childish imaginations shined brighter than the Sun before
They were stolen,
lost in a black void of expectations and reputations.

First Name

Instead of naming me Ahmed
Why not Alex?
Instead of Aziz, why not Alan?
Oliver instead of Osama?
Instead of Muhammad why not Max?
I'm tired of living with two faces on,
Not belonging to either view.
I'm told my name is a badge of honor but
what honor is there in sharing the name of a
"dead terrorist?"
What strength is there in carrying the burden of
an entire race, religion, identity on my shoulders?
What promise of *Jannah* justifies
a young boy suffering the scorn of prejudice when
all I wanted was to not be othered?

Defining Pain (i)

Pain (noun)

Definition 1: physical suffering or distress, as due to injury, illness, etc.

It's dying to shed this mold of toxic masculinity,
and straggling through a no man's land of
Meatheads and
Gym rats and
Wife beaters and
Self-absorbed jackasses;
A madhouse of madmen fueled by
rage, roids,
booze and pride.

It's the urge to smash your fist into every mirror in your house
so you don't have to stare into
Emptiness,
Ugliness,
Fear,
Failure,
Regret & remorse;

Wanting nothing more
than to shed your own skin
for something more "normal."

Harambox

Smoking is *haram,*
Drugs are *haram,*
Theft is *haram,*
Zina is *haram,*
Deception,
Treachery,
Infidelity,
Fitnah,
All *haram.*

But what's also *haram* is
Shoving Pandora's Box in a child's face and then
Damning them for opening it.

It's sin to pressure the youth till they crack,
To drown their pain in platitudes and patronization,
To crucify or exile them from love and safety so that
All they have is the void.

The Anxiety That Comes with Trying to Write about the Past

So many things to reflect and speak on; let me start with

-- Wait;

No, not that thought, it's too personal,
So I'll find another memory to feed,
Like the time when

-- Pause;

You sure you're recalling correctly?
Memories are fickle,
Can't trust all of your brain's wrinkles,
So keep on churning and churning
and eventually the right words will fall.

Words like "love," "forever," "friends"

-- Pause;

> *-- Wait;*
> *-- What?*
> *-- No —*

Those feelings don't exist anymore what makes you think you can
recollect reminisce and write and revise
when those words aren't worth a

> *-- Break;*
> *-- Refrain;*

-- Stop; -- Interrupting;

But there's no one else talking,
Just you your heart and mind
Digging away and burying ashes with
burnt hands,
holding signs
of people forgotten
but pain remaining.

Monster

Ignoring emotions, abiding cowardice,
You're insane to think you can turn your back
to a beast
And not expect it to grow more violent until
It's too strong to beat.

What you ignore will never lose sight of you.

Blindness won't kill the horror, no,
It will haunt you
until you're too impaired,
Poisoned,
Paralyzed and
powerless to stop it tearing your soul apart.

Man

Man will boast about
His strength,
His body count,
His fat stacks of cash,
His accolades and his accomplishments,
For man is conditioned to seek power and status,
And these things are his downfall.

The self-appointed leader is enslaved by his desires,
Smoking away the stress, drinking down the pain,
Lacerating with words and hands,
In the name of God and *Deen*,
Country and self, himself condemned,
For these things are his downfall.

Pity the Ummah whose men
forsake the After for the Here,
Constant craving, greed austere,
With those ideals he lies, kills, cheats, and steals,
Leaving burning fields, hollow soils behind,

Kintsugi Through a Kaleidoscope

Unaware that Earth is all-knowing, all-feeling,
And his ignorance is his downfall.

Man feigns immortality by molding his sons,
Stripping them of their hazmat suits and shove them
to terrible poisons; tobacco, toxicity, take and take,
Because tHaT's whAt ReaL mEn do,
But this will be their downfall,
Doomed to recast man's sins on
boys unborn, lands unconquered,
Time unapproached,

Unless we, men of today, stop it here and now.

Defining Pain (ii)

Pain (noun)

Definition 2: a distressing sensation in a particular part of the body.

Getting there...

It's being told as a young girl

You're overreacting;
Stop being emotional!
Watch what you wear!
X is halal but Y is haram.

It's being told to man up when you're tired of
Being so strong for too long.
It's always being judged before
Stepping out onto your own path.

It's when someone says they love you
then lies with another person behind your back.
Betrayal by your best friend, your lover,
That is a pain like no other;

Kintsugi Through a Kaleidoscope

You'll feel your brain fracture in two,
Your blood turn to acid,
Your heart corrode.

Cheaters

deserve the axe.

Communicating about relationship issues is
a sign of maturity,

To use someone as an emotional pillow and someone else as
a sex toy?
That's
        unforgivable;
It's
        unfathomable,
But you can only do so much; people are selfish.
Sometimes you must be selfish too
and tell yourself:

Cheaters deserve the axe.

A Jester among Vultures

Entertaining them,
Denying yourself,
Drunken envy and
Draining your wealth.

Rotting your mental
as you jest for them all
like a courtroom fool,
and when you least expect it:

a slip a fall,
a crack, splinters,

the vultures will pick at the fool,
till there's no more but bones,
shells, scraps,
and broken remains.

Jiniri

Just as your presence could be felt,
So too can your absence now.

No matter how many times I try to
kill the past and pick up where I left off I
still see you in another world,
dragging me back to oblivion.

I want to be rid of you, but I also want to
drown you. Again. And again.
And let you know
how much I hurt and
how much I hate.

To Forgive

Allah, the Most Glorified,
The Most High, goes by many names,
As God is many things,
But above all, God is Al-Ghafūr,
The All-Forgiving!
So who are we to deny
A brother or sister who comes to us,
Asking forgiveness for their wrongdoing
when Allah will surely forgive them?

I am Human.

I am not God
to look past another's flaws unequivocally,
I am too human to let go when asked because
I am stubborn by design, and sometimes,
To carry on, to survive, I cannot forgive.

About Anger

Anger is an abstract amalgam of scarlet and crimson,
A stampede of one for many,
Smeared,
blotched,
sprayed everywhere,
It's fire dancing wildly in a cracked vase
but with no way out,
not even up,
So all you can do is feel its bitter taste,
And wish you, like warriors wielding katanas,
Could cut down the liars,
Traitors,
Thieves and
Dictators because

To know anger is to lust for another's blood
While boiling your own,

But to know *my* anger is to implode in the night and
Spend the day undoing the damage.

Misery Economy

It costs to live,
We work to live,
In a system of greed that won't let us live;

Some of us go mad and want out,
But
it costs to die,
We work to pay bills and die for a
system that will
suck every last penny from your corpse,
long before you realize your final days.

The devil always plays tricks,
And the great lie of the American Dream,
Manifest Destiny,
Chasing money and hedonistic tendencies,
Got us drunk on our own egos,
Blind to the fact that

We're killing ourselves,
Slowly but surely,
In a system that trades in empathy for misery,

Disintegrates communities for you-versus-me,
Showers itself in paper bills, coins, blood, oil,
All to make a monster of humanity.

The Failed State:

Gives thoughts and prayers to national tragedies,
While conducting worldwide atrocities;

Squeezes bodies for blood and sweat,
Land for oil and drugs, gaslights the martyrs,
Praises their perfect soldiers —

Discards those bodies (expendable) with glee,
For younger, fresher generations of killers-to-be;

Shuffles the boogeymen like a deck of cards,
Fear and hysteria are the empire's bodyguards;

Is birthed by violence, grows by violence,
Spreads violence, yet condemns violence;

Values guns over kids,
Doctrine over women's bodies,
Shackles the spirit, for prison pays;
Lies about the state of its soul,

Masking evil as sainthood, false royal,

Starves the body to line the pockets,
As warmongers fire off the rockets.

The failed state is a pitiful state,
And we, the cogs, are worn out and tired.

God help us rebuild from a failed state.

Rueing

One of my biggest regrets is
Not holding a mirror to your tyranny,
So that even if you are not mortified,
You understand why
You will fall.

Fighting for Consciousness

True strife is when you
wake every morning fighting the urge to
go back to bed,
eyes closed, mind shut,
numb and oblivious to the fog of war
clouding your vision, your dreams,
your ray of sunshine.

Sometimes,
Some of us wake,
Fighting the urge to never want to
wake again.

If you've felt this way I just want to say:
despite the fact so many will never understand,
I know you don't want to go on feeling this way.
No, you're not crazy, despite what they may say,
and I hope you see, in spite of your perceived brokenness,
Your beauty is grand.

I Hate the Winter

I. Hate. The. Winter.
Hate it with a passion as burning as a scorching summer sun.

Birth, Life, Death, Decay.
Spring, Summer, Autumn, Winter.
Death alone is hard enough to think about,
Without that grueling image of
immolation to appease the cycle of seasons,
"Ash to ashes, dust to dust,"
I don't need or want a reminder that
All things beautiful fade to blank.

How can I not hate the winter
when I miss the warm embrace of the sun?
when I long for the wind's soft touch?
when I miss long walks?
when I long for rooftop sunsets?
Beach trips?
Long days and longer nights?
Life outside the walls?
And rather than freeze, just stay chilling?

AHMED AYOUB

Winter is creative kryptonite,
Amplifying the anxiety,
Petrifying the process,
Days of radiance reduced to fleeting moments.

Seasons change and so do the demons;
Longer nights mean longer fights
with bigger frights and no end in sight. See:
The road to Hell is paved with good intentions but
isn't it better to walk,
to walk through that fiery road, reach the end,
look back and say
"I learned?"
Sure as hell beats freezing up in place,
swapping my blood pump with a block of ice.

I'm already trying to accept that like the autumn leaves,
things fall apart.
And funny enough,
Winter, like vengeance
will always serve reminders of how
cold, dark, and lonely it all can really be...

Till next season.

Harb ("War")

Never changes...
No matter on what grounds,
or in whose minds.

No one wins in the aftermath,
Not the earth marred by craters,
Nor the homes reduced to rubble,
Not the innocent plagued by strife,
Nor the brain collapsing on itself.

Scars carry weight,
Between piles of bricks,
Crises of faith,
Lost shelters and lost self
— irreparable —
With innocence being the first casualty,
Then all
          other
layers
          fall.

In the deepest trenches,

AHMED AYOUB

Even an atom's weight of
faith may be your greatest weapon,
And all one can do is pray,

> Grant me power,
> So that I may
> Overcome my mortal enemies and
> Destroy my inner demons,
> So that I may yet live,
> To see another sunrise,

Grasp a shred of hope,
And look through the haze
for a chance to

r
  e
    b
      u
        i
          l
            d.

Prodigy, Pariah

Great expectations
enforced by —

grades,
image,
perception,
dress code,
yessirs, no ma'ams,
stay quiet,
respect your elders,

— sap the creativity,
the will of individuality,
rendering an unconscious corpse,
moved by approval, academic achievement,
a name to prove, discouraged from passions early on.

The child prodigy
burdened by —

weights of

AHMED AYOUB

old legacies
in new lands,

— Is taught to be good in school,
and doors will swing open;

Is told they have a reputation to uphold,
in the face of eyes back home, and
faces of post-9/11 ignorance;

Is shamed for their name in school,
their religion on the news,
their skin in media,
suffering death-by-one-thousand-obtuse-pundits,
a trial of predetermined guilt: 'otherness;'

The child prodigy —

feeling less and less welcome,
carrying one world on their back
while lifting another in their grip,

— Begs for reprieve from these pressures,
A chance at withdrawal, then is
let go, falling into an abyss of stagnant apathy.

The prodigy, child no more,
    stripping the grades, accolades, titles, and honors,
                has lost their way, malady of marvel,
with nowhere to turn but inwards,

regresses to recluse,
unaware that a contest of wills has begun...

II.

Messiness

Pariah, Prodigy

Who am I?
What was I born for?
What are my strengths?
Hopes? Fears? Failures?
Wants? Needs? Desires?

Where do I start?

I need a place to start,
I need to find myself,
the 'me' behind the prodigy, the pariah,
to kill my old self on my own terms,

And one day,
The shut-in will shed all traces of their
sheltered self,
Embracing the vagabond soul,
Leaving their chasm behind to
see the world anew, born anew,
to become a prodigy of endless possibility.

Ketamine

Entrance me in aphrodisia,
Shoot me sky high,
Let us melt together and
freeze up time.

Hide me from the light,
Open up oblivion,
Burst me into flames and
drag me down to the trenches.

Shock my systems,
Blow my mind,
Fill me up so much that I
can't pour into myself.

Forced Growth

Trauma forces us to grow up
in the blink of an eye, but rarely
— if ever —
does it let us grow outward
without a fight.

Polarity

The dichotomy between pleasure and pain
is as clear as sun versus rain.

Such is the wave of the universe,
circling between birth, life, death, and decay.

Where friendship can evolve into matrimony,
Inner peace can devolve to catastrophe.

I, a bystander, a grain of sand,
am blown around by a chaotic wind;
Maybe God's way of pushing me to act?
Maybe an illusion of relocation
only to find that the more things change,
the more they stay the same.

Fatigue

Life needs to stop for like a week;
Just freeze everything up because I'm feeling so weak and
Sick to the stomach, heart so heavy,
Dealing alone in the diaspora.

Lord give me strength, lend me your guidance and
Help me make sense of this in the midst of the silence
Because they say that silence is so loud it's deafening, so
What can I do to stop all of the screaming?

Matter of fact, please help me to turn back time
So I could find an entirely different mountain to climb.
New faces,
New places, and
Going through difference phases;
Rewriting a life with no regrets in these pages.

Your Own

Sometimes, when you don't expect it,
Your own are the reason; the
rotten bastards will
Lie
Cheat
Steal
Look away
Stay silent
Plug their ears or
Bury their heads
before they put themselves
on the front lines
with you.

When you're tired and beaten,
No backup in sight,
You'll then realize that,
they tossed you to oblivion,
Like scraps to the dogs.

Defining Pain (iii)

Pain (noun)

Definition 3: mental or emotional suffering or torment.

The worst enemy is the invisible one.

They don't tell you it's the urge to disembowel yourself
because if you can't take life as a man, maybe you can
take death like one.

They don't tell you it's this physically non-existent but
metaphysically omnipotent cage;
Your mind a prison, your heart the watch guard,
Your soul the prisoner.

Dear Chester,

Sometimes words don't do justice to someone's presence, and much less often define what they mean to those who love them. Near and far you led with love, spoke truth to soul, screamed like a devil and sang like an angel. You were and will forever be one of the true underdog stories, but we wish your journey didn't end.

You made so many see and respect the power of the mind and your absence screams, louder than your lyrics ever could, now and forever. Sometimes words do no justice to someone's presence because we stand in awe and amazement at their raw sincerity, their capacity for empathy and their stories of survival.

But now all that's left is a vacuum that can't be filled, and to this day I hope you understand that when your light went out,
In the end,

We all cared.

A Regret

Oftentimes we take what we love
for granted,
And when it's gone, we spend Years
chasing the ghosts, asking
for forgiveness,
for one more chance.

Fog

Words spoken and written dissolved like
Words in my head,
Memories colliding like atoms but
Never bonding together,
Just as if I'm living separate from myself —

I remember old friends and good times,
Their faces now deformed by envy, wrath,
Greed and bitter contempt.

In speaking my story, time and time over,
I've lost words of a home away from home,
Stuck between here and there with little direction,
Hazed through the motions without much purpose.

If we are beings of light,
Then why am I unseen in this fog?

Living Grief

Your greatest joy can,
In the blink of an eye,
With the speed of a squall,
And the fury of a forest fire,
Mark your life,
And become your greatest sorrow.

Maybe they were never who you needed,
Maybe they've lost part of themselves,
Maybe they've become a shell of their past,
Stuck trying to create something from nothing —

And grief feeds on nothingness,
Fills itself on emptiness,
And if you let it, it will feed on you too.

But then...

Maybe you weren't who they needed, now,
At this point in time.
Maybe you lost yourself too,

Giving everything to another without
Letting life flow into you,

Maybe we both got swept up in nothingness,
And letting go let all the grief break in,
And now it feeds on us too.

For how long, who's to say?

Defining Pain (iv)

For each of these paths of pain, there are
roads of reconciliation and hallowed hopes:

Maybe you ought to detox your own perception of others —

Maybe these 'perfect people' on magazine covers
are the ugly ones —

Who are you to leech away youthful energy
and shackle their spirits? —

Love your "loved ones" more. Or at least just
learn to love them at all —

You never know what someone carries, so be kind,
as you will need kindness returned —

And seek to understand someone's pain
instead of mocking them.

Above all,
The warrior's pain, forged in fire and strife,
Will always,

and forever,
overshadow people's ignorance and pride.

The Withering Rose Still Stands

My eyes screamed to be free of me,
Overworked, drowned, overnight
into the daylight hours,
But, as I must,
Suffered the pain of loss.

Day by day, with what little life remains I
stare myself down in the mirror,
Streams now darkened and dried,
Give o'clock shadow now striking midnight,
A husk, sick with an obscure sorrow, an
emptiness after a
long stretch of love,
Looking beyond, to solace of an
"and then,"

My face cowered in, burying itself,
But how can I face the day without
Facing myself?

Kintsugi Through a Kaleidoscope

How much more time will I
Squander away, petrified? —

No, not this time, not again.

Now breathe.

I must embrace the day by its hours,
The hour by its minutes,
The minute by its seconds,
And unwrinkle and once again look lovingly
Into that mirror, greeting a better me,

And I'll start by resetting the clock.
I will shed the reminders of a now-past life
from my face,
To grow again into someone new,

For the withering rose still stands.

Delta

I walked the bridge
into the concrete jungle.
But to make my own way through it all I
didn't have the luxury of space,
Security,
Safety.

Cut in half, and now up ahead,
Trying to balance myself
above crashing waves,
I'm terrified to cross,
But it's: do that and risk
falling or: accept it and drown in the noise.
And so I trek to the other side,
One, two, fearful blindness,
Left, right, willful ignorance.
Just enough to get through
and not fall to my doom.

Barely visible,
Between you and me lies a narrow walk;

Kintsugi Through a Kaleidoscope

A tight rope between permanent collapse and a
fistful of goals that
no amount of gold can buy.
But I'm tired of being the fall guy,
Never having an alibi for why I don't
walk that thin line;
I'm stranded sky-high unable to reach
the other tower, feeling like the end is nigh.
Crazy thing is I know that ain't true,
So I walk that rope, balanced by my truth,
Reconciling whatever end this comes to.

Litany of Temperance

I am ethereal in physical form,
Unbound by my sins and failures,
For battles lost are lessons learned.

My emotions are my humanity,
I will let them come into me, sit a while,
Pass through me, and leave me refreshed.

I carry hurt and regret yet
I will untangle this barbed web to
Let others in, free of that pain, free to nurture.

I acknowledge I will falter and tire,
And find myself in echo chambers of silence,
But I will use this space to revitalize...

For I am a storm,
And the calm.

III.

Rebuilding

Inertia

The more things change,
The more they stay the same,
Till you realize you're stuck in the same
Mindset
Routine
Space
Rotten
Stale
Decaying
Cobwebs
Dust
Abandoned but
Occupied by something you don't
recognize when you look in the mirror:

What they may call indolence, you live out as a
Fight for a breath, a pulse, a beat,
Something, anything,
Because it all has to change, some way,
Somehow.

Mind's Eye to God

Now I think I'm starting to see,
Maybe God isn't failing humanity.
Maybe
our earthly insanity
makes us think this way.

Luna Reflected

Some nights consume you,
Lonely mind wandering while
The moon laments too.

But for Ramadan,
She engulfs all the darkness
and faith is reborn.

Break the Ceiling

You've spent so much time looking up and
seeing the sky shatter and fall that
you lose sight of the fact that you're
still standing on your own two feet,
still on solid ground;
A base,
A foundation,
A way up
Against a broken sky,
Till you eventually come face to face with
Venus herself.
And in that moment, I hope you realize that
all you ever needed was right at your feet,
lifting you up.

Senses

I wish orchids would grow on the streams of
tears you've shed over the years,
If only to see how beautiful you have always been.

I wish you could see the light of the moon as
I gaze into your eyes, darker than black,
If only to realize how profound your insight has always been.

I wish everything you touched turned into platinum,
If only to understand how invaluable you are,
How you've touched and enriched so many lives.

Afraid to Start

I wish I didn't sink trying to
float my feelings to paper,
left breathless by the crushing weight of
everything I want to say and
too afraid to breathe life into it all.

But I must.

Honor Your Work

Love your grind but don't glamorize it.
Your struggles make you,
But be careful what they mold you into.

What motivates you will eventually
Feed off of you.

What you love may not
love you back,
But we must say and make and do and live
to give love, not to demand it.

Respect your hustle but don't
Melt your mind, body, and soul for
A newly minted title,
A sense of control,
Ownership of people, places, and things,

For what motivates you will eventually
Feed off of you.

Forget Them Now

Forget those who

(choose to)

forget you:

You're sitting alone in a
Charcoal forest with no hope except
to burn,

Burn that list of used-to-be's;
Friends, family, lovers,
Memories, photographs, and
Sentimental accessories,

Until all that's left is a
level playing field,
a fresh start,
a new horizon ahead.

Healing

Let me paint you a picture of
What it's like to rebuild and recoup the Self
with my blood, sweat, and tears,

It's looks of misery, anger, disdain, sadness
in the mirror,
It's self-doubt whispering loudly in the silence:
you can't do it why bother?
It's relapsing through the same nonsense,
And though you've lost count you'll swear
It'll never happen again.

It's floating through days and nights then
without warning,
Crawling with mountains on your back,
the acid in your throat,
and fear in your skin.

It's longing for a piece of you that you left behind
while knowing that looking back is like
staring Medusa in the eyes.
It's taking a second, a third, a tenth

Kintsugi Through a Kaleidoscope

Look in the mirror and seeing a seed growing,
A body evolving,
A soul flowing like the blood in your veins,
The sweat on your forehead,
The tears down your face.
It's growth because life demands it and
It's growth in spite of those who
tried to stuff you into a crypt.

It's trial by fire,
And only the finest and sharpest swords
Are forged in fire.

Three Day Turn

Day 1 —
He draped his excitement over his fear,
Like a dark blue peacoat,
And even as he first laid his eyes on her
he couldn't help but tremble inside;
She seemed calm, quiet, composed, tired,
but just as lovely as he'd expect,
and adore her he did, in silence and glances.

Day 2 —
A brief embrace to warm the spirits
on a cold rainy winter day,
Walking aimlessly, getting lost together, staring at art,
Secretly admiring each other in
unseen glances and photos;
A slippery fall, arms interlocked,
from makeup to dinner
He enjoyed the long walk.
A dim-lit restaurant, just the two of them,
As she talked and recalled, he sat there, in admiration,
a twinge of awe.

Kintsugi Through a Kaleidoscope

One more trip together, and he wanted her to know,
If the ride got rough he wouldn't let her go.

And I think she knew,
in the way their hands fit together.

Day 3 —
He'd prepared for this day since before he'd seen her,
But how do you part ways with someone who feels
like a part of you?
A sunny and chilly afternoon on a porch,
And all he cared about was her head resting on him,
Arm around her,
Hand in hand, locked tight.
A ride to the airport, and the melancholy settles in,
But while she's on the phone her hand
sneaks back into his,
And he couldn't help but smile,
squeezing that hand tight.

Bags checked in, and it's time to say goodbye,
But he didn't want to let her go.
And while they both had no choice,
They couldn't just leave with parting words;
When the nervous joy settled he pressed his lips to hers,
felt her warmth, took it all in,
and struggled even more to let her go.

And since that moment,

AHMED AYOUB

They could only pray that next time,
Three days would turn to three weeks.

What Have I Learned from a Love That Ended?

That the little things matter a lot more,
More than the grandiose, and
They're a lot harder to notice than you think.

Expectations, hopes, and dreams
All run rampant like wildfires,
If left unchecked.

Reminders come in all shapes and sizes,
Flavors and sounds,
Scents and dreams;
You bear the pain all over again,
All the while smiling at the joy you lived.

Emotions in the aftermath are most intense,
Ever difficult to control,
And in those times it's vital to give them space,
Space to scream them out,
Space to sleep them off...

Just as fast as it sets you ablaze,
So too can time pass,
Until you realize you're standing on wood
and it's too late.

Grief transcends death;
It lives in those newfound permanent absences.

Balance matters,
Between togetherness and solitude,
Compromise and contest,
For love cannot flourish unchallenged,
A heart crushed by fear, no nourishment,
No rest.

Time shoved life onward,
And in time, believe it or not, you will move too.
It won't be in a day, not a week,
Nor month nor maybe even years,
But you will, one day.

I never thought I could love and could
Be loved so,
I believe that however unlikely,
Love will find its way to each of us,
Where we may unravel into another's
Loving embrace,
For love moves life,
And in time, you will move on.

Fulfill

I know who and what I deserve,
So whether I'm alone at the table or not,
I will keep on dining and feasting
on the fruits of life until
Death satisfies my hunger.

Catalysts

Through my elders, I learned to fear God,
Through my enemies, I learned to seek God,
Through my Ummah, I learned to resent God,
Through my friends, I learned to return to God,
Through you, I learned to remember God,
Through you, I learned to thank God,
Through you, I learned to love God.

Moving through many paths of pain,
Freighted with burdens and traumas,
Leading up to this moment in time,
in this space, in such a presence,
It was worth it —
You are worth it.

Flow

The marble statue stood steadfast
against the pounding of the sea,
beaten and lashed by wave after wave,
yet unwavering facing unfettered scorn,

Yet time alters all before it,
and marble is chipped,
cracked,
etched and
maimed,
lost to winds and waters,
until marble no longer stands but
is scattered in the flow of the world.

But,
what if the stone giant needed to
lose form,
move with nature's hand guiding it,
to new paths and greater forms?

Verse Alchemy

There's anxiety that comes with writing about the past
but see,
The beauty in words is that you create meaning,
Something whole born from chaos,
Gaining power of truth and truth of power,
Until you find yourself transmuting
thoughts to verses that rhyme, collide,
amplify voices and battle the dark side,

See the power of these words as I
Unravel my thoughts and let them fly —
Take my pain, my joy, my rage, my hope,
Transposing sounds from lands nears and far,
mixing and blending so you get
A matrimony or emotions
Giving voice to the unheard!

You too have that power, just look within, and
Let your being flow into words yet unseen.

Syzygy

They may not understand,
May not care to, may pretend not to but
Solis sees,
Luna hears,
Terra feels,
Why you water the land with your sweat and tears,
Or beat it with your feet and fists,
Why you walk on,
Or stay still, steadfast or spread out.

When you gaze up at that expansive black or blue,
what do you see?
what do you hear?
what do you feel?

You are infinitely fractional,
A flicker in the space of the endless void,
Yet in that infinite smallness lies ubiquity,
A great power locked, and you have the key.

If no one else understands,
Know that these words do;

They know why you fight,
That you strive to live,
That one day, the splendor of
Your soul will spark the way
For you, for me, for us, for fate.

Divine Omnipotence has decreed that
The strong endure the pain,
So I know you'll face each day somehow,
And in spite of your trials,
You'll open the door to tomorrows until
One day, you walk through the door,

And you'll look back knowing that
Everyone and everything needed to happen,
Because, well, life's funny that way,
And fate, in hindsight, follows a perfect path,
And in that path, you experienced
All that you needed to grow beyond.

IV.

Scars of Gold

Alternative Undoings

In another universe,
Rachel Corrie would be married, with kids,
Columbine would just be another typical high school,
Saudi Arabia wouldn't be holy in name only,
Hiroshima wouldn't be synonymous with "bomb"
And never in any corner of the world
would we see a Nazi.

Not another Black body lifeless nor
Trails across borders and oceans,
carrying pain and trauma,
broken dreams and English,
To lands conquered, whitewashed, drained of soul,
I could walk the steps of al-Aqsa with
A black-white-green-red flag
Hoisted high, pointing towards Allah as if to say,
"Your Lord has not abandoned you."

And yet we must wrestle with the daily realities,
The current streams of horror that flood
our collective conscience;

Kintsugi Through a Kaleidoscope

I look to the sky each day and hope, one day,
By the dawn, and the night,
that alternative dreams become
grounded realities.

Oscillation

I'm a man of science but I hate subscribing to
the notion of oscillation
    And I'm not talking about ping-ponging between the ups
and downs,
        I'm talking about how we open up and grow with
people,
            Strangers we knew nothing about fitting the mold of
                Friend;
          Family;
          Fiancée;
    For all that to fall back down and circle back around to
Strangers;
Silence;
    Semblances of sorrow,
      But the silver lining still shines
        Because theories aren't facts but this
will always ring true:
           You are your only constant.

Birthright

I got words for the half-assed,
Half-hearted,
Half-baked,
Half-here,
Closed-ear,
Half-seeing
Bastards I ain't feeling:

Stay in your lane and don't try to explain
what you think is right when you ought to refrain,
Because my insight's my greatest birthright, SO
follow along because I'm saying this once:
If you're trying to foil my vision, get out of my way,
Just take your head and go stick it in the soil.

If anyone demands you doubt your intuition you
Ignore that statement and give them this rendition: You
Spit at the notion & tell them they can eat shit because
frankly,
Who are THEY to make you fold?

Qowa ("Strength")

Treat what you hold dear as a source of
Strength, for one day, all this pain and hurt will be
Undone, one day you'll realize that all
You needed was within because of
Some and in spite of others —

Stay your course, accept love,
And you'll come into a brand-new powerful You.

Feeling Spring

Take care and guard the friendships that
feed on each person's creativity
Because the world's got enough
trendy goons and insta-buffoons,
But not enough lovers looking to understand the Soul's roots.

Maybe one day I can open your windows
And you'll learn to let the sun in
and the air through,
That joyful bellow out,
and that gleaming look of aspiration,
a passion for what lies ahead.

Artist's Love

People are temporary;
Art is eternal, as is
The Soul.

Find love in the eternal.

Don't Stop Creating

What people harshly criticize is a
reflection of their unrealized dreams;
So dear writer, keep writing,
keep filming, director,
keep rocking out, musician,
keep drawing, artist,
move like water, dancer,

Breathe life with your art.

Re: Freedom

To be too free is no better than being too trapped;
It's to choose between
being suspended in the sky with wax wings knowing
Sol and Gravity may decide to snatch it all away
at any moment,
or
being conditioned to be content with where you are,
settling because the cage is your electroshock therapy;
'You know freedom is dangerous, you could fry yourself,
if you attempt it!'

But, in this world of dualities,
one cannot be felt without the other,
As how love cannot be understood without hate.

Still, how I wish to be free.
I've only tasted a sample of that euphoria like
the first meal after a Muslim breaks their fast
on a summery Ramadan evening,
but how many more times must my stomach
have to eat itself before I can get another taste?

Kintsugi Through a Kaleidoscope

In those brief moments, I couldn't describe how powerful,
how liberating that freedom feels;
It's like accepting you're not the degenerate
because they're a disloyal coward.
It's like filtering out a large crowd of people to concentrate it
down to a concrete collective of the best friends
a man could ever hope to have...

It's like letting go of a toxic environment and being given
a chance to breathe in the brisk air, the flowers,
being caressed by the sun's radiance.

I long for that feeling where I can embrace the rain,
fully, presently,
Not from the perspective of the wax-winged fool
tangled in the thunderclouds,
And certainly not from the perspective of
the trapped & tortured captive,
devoid of spirit,
blind to everything outside that electric cage.

How I wish to be free to feel, from the fear of pain,
to just live and love without sacrifice, unconditionally.

Love

Love transcends
emotion and
chemicals, it's
a choice,
a process,
a cosmic binder,
a life-sustaining infinity,
endlessly flowing, yet serenely stilling.

Unbreakable

You can't break me;
I've thrown myself at the wall and cracked,
I've been dropped and smashed to bits,
Crumbled and shredded,
Snipped and cut,
Ground and trashed,

Yet I stand here,
Glued, taped, cemented,
Held by the universe's embrace and my own rage,
Far more powerful than you can imagine!

A New Dawn

I stared at God and
Not a damn thing mattered here...
This must be freedom!

Like the Sun,
I will rise again to reclaim
my Mantle in the Sky.

Memo to the Kid That Can't Hang

Dear Boy,

If you stick around for the whole ride,
You'll see down the road that how you look
won't get you as far as how straight you shoot,
How tall you walk,
How kind you are,
Or how you refused to give up in spite of it all.

One day you'll look in the mirror and realize that
while the thick beards,
Slick fades, pompadours,
Ice cold facades, and
Bread chasing look cool you'll only starve yourself;
Body, mind, and soul can only survive on a balanced diet of
Love,
Courage,
Vulnerability and
Ambition.

What you hate about yourself —
Those quirks, talents, habits and thoughts,
What you've been taught are weaknesses —
Those tears, hugs, the affection and gentleness,
They say those things will tear you down but
Believe me little one,
When they say you can't hang,
Take those words and with them,
Build your own playground, show them you can,
And welcome those who need a place to be.

Acknolwedgments

It often takes a village to make one's dreams come true. This book has been a dream of mine for years, and those who have touched it during the process are the reason it has come true.

I want to first thank my high school English teacher, Mr. Don Delo, for opening my soul to the world of literature. In a world before his guidance, writing and reading amounted to schoolwork. Since his classes, they have become my gateway to infinity.

Thank you to my dear friend Jessica Perez for graciously taking on the task of revising my messy thoughts and words to tighten the messages and enhance their quality. You're amazing at what you do!

I express gratitude to my parents and my sister, who never stop loving me during my silences and slumps, and for encouraging me to pursue what I enjoy more.

Thank you to many others, current and former friends. Whether you're still in my life, departed, distant, or no longer in my life for one reason or another. All the thoughtful comments, feedback, suggestions, and encouragement helped shape this dream and create it.

Eternal gratitude to the other poets and artists of the world, past and present, whose creativity helped inspire and invigorate my own creative energy.

Acknolwedgments

Lastly, I have to thank God for the ability to see this dream come to life in your hands, dear reader.